NEW OBJECT LESSONS
FOR CHILDREN OF ALL AGES

Sheryl Bruinsma

BAKER BOOK HOUSE
Grand Rapids, Michigan

Copyright 1980 by
Baker Book House Company
ISBN: 0-8010-0775-5

First printing, March 1980
Second printing, February 1981
Third printing, August 1982
Fourth printing, December 1983
Fifth printing, February 1985

Printed in the United States of America

To
my husband, Walter, and
our children,
Deborah, Rebekah, Sarah, and Peter

Contents

HOW-TO SECTION

Messages for the Children in Church

The traditional way to begin a book is with a preface or introduction. These words are usually read as "skip this and get to the real material." However, one of the purposes of this book is to broaden the reader's perspective on object lessons. It is, therefore, important to consider the many uses of object lessons and some helpful hints on how to present them.

All of the object lessons in this book have been given at least once in a church service. They have been revised to exclude awkward material and include the wonderful insights a person receives when a task is over and he or she sits down.

There are different ways to present a children's sermon. I prefer to have the children remain in their seats for the following reasons:

1. A children's sermon is training in church worship. Church worship for most adults takes place in the pew. When we bring children to the front of the church for the children's sermon and then send them back to their seats we are essentially saying, "This is your time and place to listen and participate. Afterwards you can go back to your seat and tune out."

2. Some children are too shy or consider themselves too old to come forward and are thus deprived of participation.

3. When children are brought to the front of the church they become a source of entertainment, detracting from the impact of the lesson.

4. When children remain in their seats the person giving the children's sermon is obliged to use larger objects and display them so that everyone can see them. In this way everyone is included; it becomes a family time in church.

PRESENTATIONS BY TEACHERS AND YOUTH LEADERS

These object lessons can be used in a Christian school classroom or chapel service. They can also be used as Sunday school starters and daily vacation Bible school lessons. A class teacher can set up a lesson, challenge the students, and assign them to follow through on the concept. The children can report their experiences to each other during the next class.

A teacher can also use object lessons with moral implications in the public school classroom. Classroom situations themselves are usually the source of material for teaching patience, friendship, cheerfulness, consideration, and so on. But there are times that a teacher prefers to plan such instruction in advance rather than waiting for the situation to arise. It is also easier to involve all students in a planned lesson.

PRESENTATIONS BY CHILDREN

Object lessons give a child (preferably fifth grade and up) a wonderful opportunity to read, prepare, and present his or her own lesson. It is an excellent experience in reading, following directions, drawing conclusions, speaking in front of others, and assuming responsibility for a task. Students in one class can prepare together, present to each other to gain confidence and learn from each other's lesson, and then give the lesson to another class. In this way children can learn from each other.

Consider these places for implementation:
Sunday school
Christian school devotionals
youth groups
daily vacation Bible school
junior church
family gatherings

PRESENTATIONS BY PARENTS

The art of parenting involves meeting our responsibilities in raising our children as considerate children of God. Object lessons can be read or presented in times of family sharing as an interesting and creative way to accomplish this goal. A listing of the object lessons according to their readability (grade level at which children should be able to read them) is provided on p.—, so you will know which lessons your children can be expected to read.

DELIVERING AN OBJECT
LESSON

PREPARATION
1. Read the lesson and become familiar with the concept.
2. Pray for God's guidance.
3. Consider the age, interests, and needs of the audience. This will determine the vocabulary, length, and complexity of what is taught.

4. Locate or make the object for the lesson, or select one like it which will allow for a similar message. Practice using the object so it will not hold any surprises for you when you are delivering the lesson.
5. Contemplate the lesson. Make sure it is something *you* want to say. Change it to fit your situation or personality.
6. Make an outline to include your changes. There are times when you will want to use the outline provided.
7. Prepare a smooth opening sentence so you will feel comfortable about your beginning.
8. Write out a challenging final statement. It is important to draw the lesson to a meaningful conclusion.
9. Practice the entire object lesson aloud until your own words come naturally and you no longer need to depend on the outline.

PRESENTATION
1. Hold up the object. This takes attention away from you and makes you feel less self-conscious.
2. Go through the lesson as you have prepared it—without notes. Do, however, keep your outline and opening and closing sentences within reach if you get stuck. This is good security.
3. Try to look each child in the eye at least once. Involve them in the lesson. Ask them questions (in the beginning ask rhetorical questions or those calling for a nod or hand raise until you feel confident enough to deal with unexpected answers).
4. If you feel that you do not have the attention of all the children, regain it instantly by saying something like: "Now watch this object carefully!" "Do you know what is going to happen next?" "Don't miss this!" "Look!"
5. Deliver your concluding challenge, and *stop*! Resist the impulse while you gather your things and sit down to fill in the pause with distracting comments. Let people think about what you have said.

IMPORTANT:
Remember that the purpose of an object lesson is to teach a Christian concept. Do not allow yourself to spend more than half of

the time describing the object. Make sure the children understand the concept you are teaching. Young children need to have the idea repeated several times. It might be advisable to ask them at the conclusion of the lesson what they are going to remember. It is easy to get carried away with an interesting object, but if the object is all that the children can remember, you have not accomplished your purpose.

Readability Index

"Readability" is an estimate of the approximate difficulty of reading material. A readability index tells you at which grade level an average child might be expected to read and understand a passage.

Readability is determined by computing the length and complexity of the sentences and the difficulty of the words. The nature of the concepts involved must also be considered. Sentences are counted and examined, words are sorted into "easy" and "hard" lists, and an overall estimate of the difficulty of the concept is made. It is not an easy process, but there are mathematical formulas and graphs for this purpose.

Readability is also influenced by factors which affect the individual child but are not constant and, therefore, not measurable. Some children read words easily but have difficulty putting them together into meaningful sentences. Others may labor through the passage, need assistance with several words, but still understand what they have read. In every classroom there is a wide range of reading ability. A child who is interested in the material and wants to read it may well read a passage estimated to be beyond his grade level. (The opposite is also true, that if a child is not interested he may have difficulty with material below his grade level.) For example, a child who is familiar with words such as *fellowship, community, courage, honesty,* and so on will find it easier to read the material in this book. A child who has heard many object lessons will begin to get a feel for them, and the comparisons between object and spiritual lesson will be less difficult.

Understanding the use of an outline is a skill which must be learned. If your child has not yet acquired this skill, either skip the outline or teach him to use it as a summary of the contents of the lesson.

As you can see, there are many factors involved in determining whether a child can successfully read a passage. The following list will, however, give some indication of which lessons would be appropriate for your children.

OBJECT LESSONS

1.

A NEW SEASON

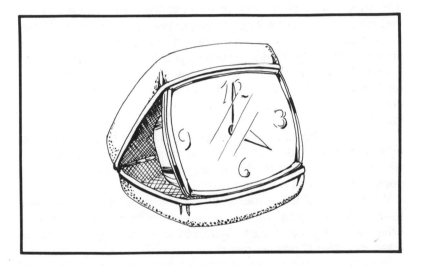

OBJECT: An alarm clock (a fold-up travel alarm adds interest but is not necessary for the lesson).

LESSON: We should take an active part in a new season.

TEXT: "Wake up, sleeper, and rise from death, and Christ will shine on you" (Eph. 5:14b).

OUTLINE

Introduce object: Discuss the features of the alarm clock you are using.
1. The alarm rings—the new season is here.
2. You wake up—be aware that something new and important is happening.
3. You get up—become an active part of the new season.
Conclusion: Don't be caught sleeping or someday you might wake up and find out that you have missed what life is all about.

Can you guess what is in this little case? Let me give you a hint. It can make noise. Do you have an idea now? Here, I'll show you. It is an alarm clock. It folds up into this little case when you are traveling so that it will not get broken or take up much room. When it is set up, it can do what other alarm clocks do. What is the job of an alarm clock? That's right! It wakes you when it is time to get up.

The alarm rings when the new day starts. The alarm has already rung on our new season this year. It has started and you are here. I'm happy to see so many of you. I'm glad you have not missed this special day.

Sometimes the alarm rings, but we don't even hear it. We sleep right through it, and don't realize that it is time to wake up. Then we can be in a lot of trouble when we do wake up! We need to open our eyes and greet the new day.

We also need to be aware of what is happening in our new season. What things are the same? What things are different? What new things can I learn? We need to be thinking ahead about what important things we can do.

Sometimes people shut off their alarms and go back to sleep. But it is better to get up and get moving. Become a part of the action. Put yourself into the new program by singing, praying, and studying. There are many ways you can help your teacher. Perhaps you are already planning to invite a friend to church next week. (Give other suggestions appropriate to your program.)

This is going to be a great year! Don't be caught sleeping! When you wake up you might find out that you have missed what life is all about.

2.

POISON IVY

OBJECT: A poison ivy plant or a drawing of one. Use rubber gloves or tongs to hold a real one.

LESSON: Listen to the advice of responsible people.

TEXT: "Listen when I reprimand you; I will give you good advice and share my knowledge with you" (Prov. 1:23).

OUTLINE

Introduce object: Tell about an experience you have had or have heared about with poison ivy.

1. People get poison ivy because they don't know what the plant looks like, or they don't know about the rash it causes. Wise people listen to advice.
2. People get poison ivy because they don't watch where they are going. Be careful where you walk.
3. Poison ivy spreads. A bad habit or idea can take over your life.

Conclusion: Be smart; listen to good advice.

When we were on vacation this summer, we climbed over a small hill to watch a fire being put out by firemen. We were in a perfect place to see all of the action. It was fun to watch the firemen holding the hoses from the fire engine and putting out the blaze. When the fire truck was preparing to leave, we turned to walk away. I looked down and saw that we were standing in a patch of poison ivy. My son Peter was the only one with shorts on. Soon he was covered with an itchy rash.

Some people get poison ivy because they don't know what the plant looks like. Here it is. I'm holding it with rubber gloves because I don't want to have a rash like Peter had. Take a good look at this plant so you can avoid it when you are in the woods next time. If you see it, don't touch it.

You don't have to listen to my advice. You could find out about poison ivy the hard way by touching it and seeing if you get a rash. That wouldn't be very smart, though. The Bible tells us that a smart person listens to good advice. You can learn a lot from other people, especially older people who know more than you do.

People get poison ivy because they don't look where they are going. My son Peter and I know what poison ivy looks like, but we were so excited about watching the fire that we didn't pay attention to where we were going. Do you know the line from the song, "Oh, be careful little feet where you walk"? We need to be very careful where we are going—not just because our bodies might be hurt but we might "catch" bad habits and attitudes. Be aware of where you are going and what you are doing.

Poison ivy spreads when you scratch it. It can go all over your body. In the same way, a wrong idea or a bad habit can spread all through your life. To avoid this, be smart; listen to good advice.

3.

CHURCH BELLS

OBJECT: A church bell rung from the steeple, or a smaller bell, or photograph or drawing of a bell.

LESSON: We are God's messengers.

TEXT: "A reliable messenger is refreshing to the one who sends him, like cold water in the heat of harvest time" (Prov. 25:13).

OUTLINE

Introduce object: Give history of church bell usage. If possible, have bell rung for demonstration.
1. We are God's messengers to His world.
2. We bring different messages.
Conclusion: What message will you bring?

Every Sunday many churches begin the service by ringing the church bell. When I hear the bell, I often wonder what the message of the bell was to people who lived before me.

In the days when small communities were centered around the church, people depended upon the bells for messages. The bell rang joyfully for meetings, weddings, and the birth of a child. To ring a bell joyfully, the bellringer would pull the rope hard and give the bell a full swing. It would go ding-ding (pause), ding-ding. The slight pause is caused by the motion of the clapper (point to clapper on drawing) at high speed. A warning bell was a steady, medium-speed, even swing. A tolling bell was swung slowly and stopped so that the clapper only hit one side of the bell. The townspeople could hear a slow, single clang, clang, clang. When the bell tolled, it meant sorrow—usually death. This was also the way to ring the bell to signal the time. (Listen to how it was done . . .)

Just as the bell was the messenger to the village, we are God's chosen messengers to his world. He depends on us. He has given us mouths to speak about him.

We have different messages to bring. Some people become ministers. Some people become teachers. Parents bring God's message to their children. Children can invite people to church. They can bring cheerful words to other people—young and old. They can sing God's praises.

We can all ring out with a clear, helpful message. What message will you bring?

4.

HOW TO CATCH A FRIEND

OBJECT: A mousetrap.

LESSON: In order to make a friend, you have to be one.

TEXT: "When the Son of Man came, he ate and drank, and everyone said, 'Look at this man! He is a glutton and winedrinker, a friend of tax collectors and other outcasts!' God's wisdom, however, is shown to be true by its results" (Matt. 11:19).

OUTLINE

Introduce object: To catch a mouse, you use a mousetrap.
1. Trap: The mouse will not come to you; you need to trap it. To catch a friend, you must be one.
2. Bait: The mouse is drawn to the trap by the bait. When you show genuine interest in other people or let them help you, people are drawn to you.

Conclusion: A friend is a gift you give yourself.

To catch a mouse, you use a mousetrap, like this one. How many of you have ever seen a mousetrap before? You hook a piece of cheese on the trap because mice like cheese. It is the bait that attracts them. A mouse smells the cheese and comes to eat it. When he juggles the cheese, the trap snaps and catches the mouse. (Demonstrate using a spoon or clothespin for the mouse. Watch your fingers!) Would you use a mousetrap to catch a bear? No, you need the right kind of trap for what you want to catch.

There is a right kind of a trap to catch a friend, too. Jesus had many friends—followers, disciples, apostles. Why? What did he do? Jesus was a friend to many people. He went to visit them. He spent time with them. He got to know them. He was showing us that in order to have a friend, you need to be one.

Jesus also cared for other people. He was genuinely interested in them. He helped them and he let them help him. He ate dinner with them.

There is a saying on my coffee mug. It goes like this: "A friend is a gift you give yourself." When you catch a friend, you are sharing yourself with someone, and in return your friend shares himself with you. This is one of life's treasures.

5.

SLIME

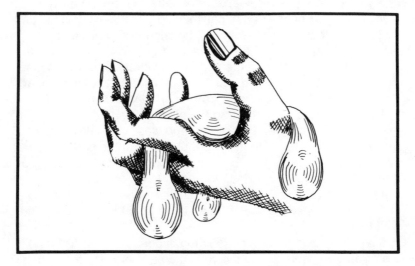

OBJECT: Slime (if the commercial "Slime" which comes in a plastic container and is sold as a child's toy is not available, use a mixture of flour, salt, water, and food coloring if desired. The concoction should be moist enough to drip slowly through your fingers when held).

LESSON: Know what you believe and stand up for it.

TEXT: "Do your best to win full approval in God's sight, as a worker who is not ashamed of his work, one who correctly teaches the message of God's truth" (II Tim. 2:15).

OUTLINE

Introduce object: This is slime—gooey, drippy, slippery slime!
1. Know what you believe.
2. Stand up for what you believe.
3. Don't go along with the crowd unless you know it is right.
Conclusion: Nobody wants to be compared with slime. God gave you a brain. Use it!

This is slime—gooey, drippy, slippery slime! Watch it slide through my fingers. It oozes in blobs. No one wants to be compared to slime. This is what we think of people who go along with everything, never thinking for themselves.

What should you do? Know *what* you believe! It isn't a belief until you have thought about it, considered it, and decided to believe it. You need to think about a statement, recognize it as true, and accept it. Then it becomes a belief. When you have decided what you believe, stand up for it. Use it in your life! If someone wants you to do something, think about whether it is the right thing to do and what will happen if you do it *before* you go along with it. Don't be afraid to say no to something you know is wrong.

Let me give you an example. You know it is wrong to swear—to take God's name in vain. So you need to stop yourself from doing it and let others know what you believe. Just because others do it, you will not be tempted to go along with them so that you can be like them. When you have made up your mind, stand up for what you believe and stick to it!

Nobody wants to be compared to slime. God gave you a brain. Use it!

6.

SLIME WITH WORMS

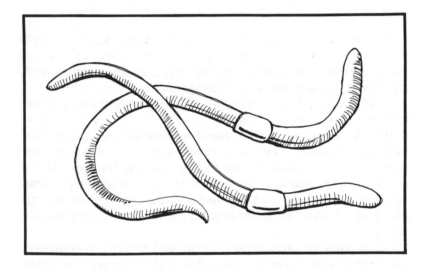

OBJECT: Slime with worms (commercially available as a toy) or a handful of earthworms.

LESSON: Go on about your life quietly and cheerfully, making the world a better place.

TEXT: "If it is to encourage others, we should do so. Whoever shares with others should do it generously, whoever has authority should work hard; whoever shows kindness to others should do it cheerfully" (Rom. 12:8).

OUTLINE

Introduce object: Be brave! Hold up the worms.
1. Worms make the earth a better place for plants to grow. We make the earth a better place for people to grow.
2. A worm has a very large mouth but does not complain. Can we say the same for people?
Conclusion: Do you need to be thanked for every little kindness you do? Does anyone ever thank the worm?

Do you remember the slime—the gooey, drippy, slippery stuff you would *not* want to be like? It also comes with worms. Yes, slime with worms! That really is an insult to these worms. They are not slimy and worthless.

The earthworm is a useful animal. He has no eyes or ears but he has a big mouth. He moves through the soil by pushing himself ahead with tiny bristles attached to the rings on his body. As he crawls along he swallows dirt and brings it to the top. In this way he is breaking up the soil so air and rain can get into it and seeds can grow. He spends his life making the earth a better place for plants to grow.

Can you say that about yourself? Do you spend your life making this earth a better place for people to grow? Does that mean that the worm may be more useful than some people?

There is something else about these worms. Remember that I said they have no eyes or ears but do have a big mouth? Well, what do most people you know with a big mouth do? Complain! Not the worm. He never complains or talks back. He goes steadily and quietly about his work doing good. If only we could be more like him—quietly and wholeheartedly going on about our lives loving Jesus, encouraging others, helping people where we can, showing kindness to those we meet, and thus making the world a better place—without complaint.

The worm does his job well, and doesn't need to be thanked. Do you need to be thanked for every little kindness you do?

7.

OPEN YOUR MIND TO WORSHIP

OBJECT: A large picture (detailed enough so that, after you have shown it, you can remove it and ask a question that most of your audience will be unable to answer).

LESSON: Worship can only occur when you actively participate.

TEXT: "Israel, you have seen so much, but what has it meant to you? You have ears to hear with, but what have you really heard?" (Isa. 42:20).

OUTLINE

Introduce object: Take a look at this picture. Ask questions about it. Ask how many times the bus stopped (see completed lesson).
1. Why don't we always see what we look at and hear what we are listening to?
   A. We are not paying attention.
   B. Like the bus question, we thought we already knew what we were going to hear, so we only listened for that.
2. We need open minds and open hearts to worship God.
Conclusion: Worship is not something that happens *to* you. It is something you must put your whole self into to enjoy.

I have a picture to show you. Look at it closely. (Hold the picture up for several seconds, then put it aside.) How many flowers (or whatever is appropriate) were in the picture? You all looked at the picture but not all of you saw everything that was in it. Perhaps you were looking for something else.

I'm going to ask you another question. Listen carefully to this riddle. A bus stopped and picked up five people. At the next stop three people got off. It stopped again and six people got on. At the next stop two people got off and one got on. It stopped again and four people got off. Now, here's the question. How many times did the bus stop? I think most of you were ready to answer a different question. You probably thought I was going to ask how many people were left on the bus.

Why don't we always see what we look at or hear what we are listening for? Sometimes we are not paying attention. It is easy to daydream when we have to sit for a long time. It takes effort to listen to what is being said. Perhaps, like the bus question, we thought we already knew what we were going to hear, so we only listened for that. We can miss a lot when we do not listen or look with an open mind.

We especially need open minds—and open hearts—to worship. Worship is praising and loving God. We Christians do many different things when we worship, and there is a purpose for these things. We pray to God and learn about him. We fellowship with other people who love him, too. But we cannot come to worship and just sit there and expect to come away feeling as if we have worshiped. We need to give of ourselves—to sing, to pray, to look, and to listen with all of our energy.

Worship is not something that happens *to* you. It is something you must put your whole self into to enjoy.

8.

YOU CAN'T JUDGE A BANANA BY ITS PEEL

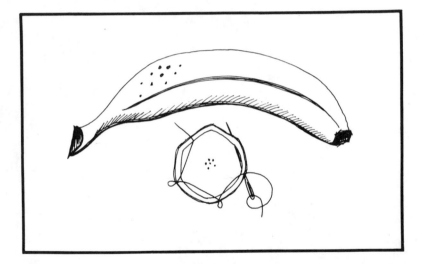

OBJECT: A specially prepared banana. (Thread a needle. Work the thread inside the unpeeled banana between the banana and the peel by "sewing" through one side of the banana and out the back. Return through the same hole and "sew" again between the skin and the banana, going out and back in through the same hole. Sew around the banana and out of the hole where you started. Gently pull the thread and it will slide through the banana, slicing it without damaging the peel. Do this in several places and the banana will be sliced when it is peeled. In a few hours the banana will be discolored where it was sliced and appear striped.)

LESSON: You must look on the inside of a person to tell what they are.

TEXT: "But the Lord said to him, 'Pay no attention to how tall and handsome he is. I have rejected him, because I do not judge as man judges. Man looks at the outward appearance, but I look at the heart'" (I Sam. 16:7).

OUTLINE

Introduce object: We all know what is inside of a banana, right?
1. This banana is different on the inside. People may be different on the inside.
2. How do we "peel" a person? We follow Jesus' example. We get to know him, help him, and love him in Jesus' name.
Conclusion: Just remember, if a banana can fool you, so can a person!

When I was young, I often heard the expression, "You can't judge a book by its cover." Do you know what that means? Well, it didn't mean much to me then, either. I brought this banana to help explain.

We all know what is inside of a banana, right? Sometimes there are some brown spots if the banana is too ripe, but this banana looks pretty good. Let's peel it and find out. (Do so.) Look! This banana is striped! And it is sliced, too! Now we certainly couldn't tell that from looking at the outside of the banana.

God tells us that he looks at the inside of people. He really knows them that way. We shouldn't think we know all about them just by seeing the outside. But we can't see people on the inside like God can. We can peel a banana, but how do you peel a person? Jesus showed us how to find out about the inside of people when he lived on earth. We can get to know them by spending time with them, helping them, and loving them in Jesus' name.

Just remember, if a banana can fool you, so can a person!

9.

BATS IN OUR BELFRY?

(HALLOWEEN)

OBJECT: A large picture of a bat.

LESSON: Prayer.

TEXT: "All of you that have reverence for the Lord and obey the words of his servant, the path you walk may be dark indeed, but trust in the Lord, rely on your God" (Isa. 50:10).

OUTLINE

Introduce object: Can you tell me what this animal is called?

I. Even though bats can see, they have a kind of natural radar that they trust to guide them. The Christian trusts God to guide him.

2. Bats make two kinds of sounds—ultrasonic sounds which guide them, and a lower-pitched voice we can hear as a squeaking sound. Christians have silent and audible prayers.

Conclusion: The next time you hear about bats, don't be afraid. Think about all of the good things we can learn from them.

Can you tell me what this animal is called? The way you answered sounds like you don't like bats. Actually, most bats are harmless. I recently heard that they make good pets. They are gentle. Out of the hundreds of different kinds of bats, only a few are harmful and they don't live anywhere around here.

Some churches are beginning to open up their steeples to give bats a place to sleep during the day because at night they go out and feast on insects. I like anything that eats insects. Maybe we, too, will have bats in our belfry!

Bats really are interesting animals. They are the only mammals that can fly. Their bodies are furry, like a mouse's. They feed their young with milk and sleep all winter like the bears. They catch insects in their mouths while they are flying.

One of the most interesting things about bats is the way they can fly in the dark. They have eyes and can see, but most bats prefer to use their natural radar. As it flies, the bat utters ultrasonic cries—too high for us to hear. The sound waves from these cries strike an object and bounce back to the bat's ears. From this the bat can tell how far away and how large the object is. If you cover a bat's eyes, it can still fly; but if you cover its mouth, it has trouble.

Christians, too, have something special to guide them. Their trust in God is like a radar which allows them to be content about the future. They know that God will protect them and show them the way to go.

Bats make two kinds of sounds. One is the high-pitched ultrasonic sound which they use to fly. The other is a lower-pitched sound which we can hear. It sounds like squeaking to us. This reminds me of the Christian also. He has two ways of praying. He can pray silently to God in his heart and no one around can hear him. Or, he can pray out loud. Often when one Christian prays out loud others pray along silently with him. Both ways are communicating with God.

The next time you hear about bats, don't be afraid. Think about all of the good things we can learn from them.

10.

SILENT LANGUAGE

OBJECT: A flip-over highway sign which is available commercially or may be constructed from cardboard and notebook rings.

LESSON: What you do may speak louder than what you say.

TEXT: "For the Kingdom of God is not a matter of words but of power" (I Cor. 4:20).

OUTLINE

Introduce object: How many of you have ever been in a car and wanted to say something to a person in another car?
1. We say things with our actions.
2. We say things with our expressions.
Conclusion: As Christians we have a message so special that people should be able to tell from what we do and even from our faces that we are different.

How many of you have ever been in a car and wanted to say something to a person in another car? But even if you shout at the top of your lungs you still can't be heard over the noise of the engines and wind. Sometimes you can say things by your facial expressions or by pointing.

This collection of signs was invented to say things to people in other cars. This sign which says, "Do you need help?" could be shown to someone who looks lost or whose car isn't running quite right. Here is a "thank you" sign to show to the person who lets your car in front of his. This one says, "Oops!" A driver can show that one when he does something he didn't mean to do. These signs are a clever way of talking without making sounds. We do this all the time without signs, but we do not always realize we are doing it.

Have you ever thought about the fact that your actions say something to other people? When you help someone, that says you like them and that you are a kind person. When you hold the door open for someone, that says you are thoughtful. When you are quiet when your teacher asks you to be, that says you respect your teacher and want to be good. I'm sure you can think of times when you have seen somebody do something unkind. What did those actions say about that person?

Have you ever said, "I'm sorry," but the expression on your face said, "No, I'm not!"? You have a choice. You can make an unpleasant task bearable with a smile, or you can undo a good deed with a frown. Your face says many things: anger, boredom, jealousy, fear, excitement, contentment, happiness. . . . Try out different expressions in front of a mirror. Find out what your face is saying to people. Remember, it is a sign you cannot put down.

Our faces show what is in our hearts. As Christians, we have a message so special that people should be able to tell from what we do and even from our faces that we are different.

11.
WHY BAPTIZE WITH WATER?

OBJECT: A glass of water, a plant, a bucket of water, and a beach towel.

LESSON: Water is significant in baptism.

TEXT: "And now, why wait any longer? Get up and be baptized and have your sins washed away by praying to him" (Acts 22:16).

OUTLINE

Introduce objects: I have four objects to show you so I have asked four helpers to hold them for me.
1. Water is necessary for life (glass of water).
   A. you can live for awhile without food but you cannot live without water.
   B. You are baptized into a new life with Christ.
2. We use water for cleaning (bucket of water).
   A. We wash to be clean.
   B. We stand fresh, clean, and forgiven in our new life.
3. Water is important for growth (plant).
   A. Without enough water, this plant will not grow properly.
   B. Our new life is one of growing and becoming more mature Christians.
4. We use water for enjoyment (beach towel).
   A. We can have a lot of fun in the water.
   B. There is joy in the love of Jesus.
Conclusion: There is a lot to think about when people are baptized. You are never too old to learn to appreciate it more.

I have four objects to show you so I have asked four helpers to hold them for me. We will explain something about why we baptize with water and what baptism means.

Peter is holding a glass of water. Water is necessary for life. You cannot live without it. You can get along without food for awhile, but you must have water for your body to work right. We use water in baptism to show that we have a new *life* with Christ.

Sarah has a bucket of water for cleaning. You would have a difficult time washing something without water. We wash ourselves, our houses, our clothes, our food . . . it seems that we are always washing something! In baptism, the water shows that we have been washed *clean*. We stand fresh and forgiven in our new life.

Rebekah is holding a plant. It needs water to grow properly. In fact, it will need a lot of water to become a big plant. When we are baptized into our new life we are not through with water. We need to continue *growing* and becoming more mature Christians. When we baptize babies, we promise to help them grow into the person God wants them to be.

This beach towel Deborah is holding reminds us that we also use water for enjoyment. Do you like to swim? We can have a lot of fun in the water. There is also a lot of *joy* in the Christian life. The more you learn about swimming the more fun you can have. So, too, our happiness as Christians grows as we learn more about Jesus and his love for us.

There is a lot to think about when people are baptized. You are never too old to learn to appreciate it more.

12.

GIVE THANKS AGAIN AND AGAIN
(THANKSGIVING)

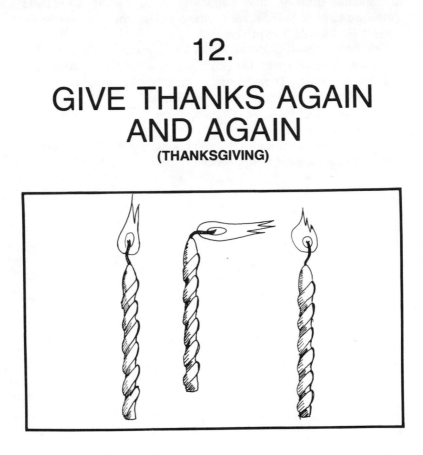

OBJECT: Trick party candles that relight when blown out.

LESSON: Thanksgiving is an attitude, not just a season.

TEXT: "In the name of our Lord Jesus Christ, always give thanks for everything to God the Father" (Eph. 5:20).

OUTLINE

Introduce object: I have some little birthday candles with me today.
1. God provides for us again and again.
2. As God provides for us, so we are to thank him.
Conclusion: I can only keep doing this with these candles until they burn out, but I can thank him now, thank him tonight, thank him tomorrow, thank him on Thanksgiving, and thank him always.

I have some little birthday candles with me today. You have all blown some like these out before, haven't you? I need a volunteer to blow these out. (Choose a volunteer). You look like you have good lungs. Try to blow them out. Try again!

There are other things we do again and again. Thanking God is one of them. Thanksgiving is a special time begun by the Pilgrims to say thank you to God. We usually have a big turkey dinner. But it is not just that meal for which we are thankful. Thanksgiving is a day to think about how many things we have been given for which we are thankful.

Thanksgiving is more than just a day or a season. God is always giving us things. We should always be thanking him. Let the flames on these candles stand for what God has given us. I will thank him (blow out). Look, he gives more. I will thank him again (blow out). He gives again. I can only keep doing this with these candles until they burn out, but I can thank God now, thank him tonight, thank him tomorrow, thank him on Thanksgiving, and thank him always.

13.

CLIMBING UPWARD

OBJECT: A large, sturdy stepladder.

LESSON: The Christian life is a process of climbing upward.

TEXT: "But continue to grow in the grace and knowledge of our Lord and Savior Jesus Christ. To him be the glory, now and forever! Amen" (II Peter 3:18).

OUTLINE

Introduce object: The Christian life is much like climbing a ladder.

1. We begin by getting on—making a decision to follow Jesus.
2. We climb slowly upward—learning more and growing as Christians.
3. We must hold on and pay attention to where we are going.

Conclusion: The more we pray and learn, the higher we climb. Are you taking a step upward today?

I have this big, strong ladder here today to help me tell you about the Christian life.

The first thing you do in climbing a ladder is to get on (step onto the ladder). You need to make a decision to get off the ground and onto the ladder. Being a Christian is not something you are born with. You need to make a decision to follow Jesus. This decision is like getting on the ladder. It is a big step!

Once you are on the ladder, you begin to climb slowly upward. The Christian also climbs upward to a fuller life as he learns more about Jesus and how to enjoy his love. Nobody ever knows all there is to know, so we climb and climb, always reaching for the top.

As we go up the ladder, it sometimes gets a little shaky. We need to hold on tightly to God's promises. We have temptations, and sometimes we may lose our footing and slip backwards a step or two. But if we hold on tightly and pay careful attention to what we are doing and where we are going, this is not likely to happen.

The more we pray and learn, the higher we climb. Are you taking a step upward today?

14.

JINGLE BELLS
(ADVENT)

OBJECT: Jingle bells, one for each child. Inexpensive bells can be tied with a string so they ring.

LESSON: Clearly ring out the news that Christmas means God sent his son for us.

TEXT: "She will have a son, and you will name him Jesus— because he will save his people from their sins" (Matt. 1:21).

OUTLINE

Introduce object: I have a jingle bell for each of you.

1. The bells make a happy sound. We are happy God sent his son for us.
2. Each bell has a little clapper inside. Our message comes from our hearts.
3. Your bell will not ring when something touches it. Do not crowd your Christmas and dull the real meaning.

Conclusion: Take your jingle bell home and let it remind you this whole Christmas season what Christmas is really about.

I have a jingle bell for each of you. It is going to tell us something we want to remember this Christmas season. See if you can hold your bell still until everyone gets one and then we'll ring them together.

Ready? Hold your bell by the string and let's all ring them. Isn't that a happy sound! The first thing these bells tell us is that Christmas is a happy time. We are happy because Christmas is a time we celebrate that God sent his son for us. How much he loves us to have sent his son! We are happy because Christmas means that Jesus was born.

Look closely at your bell. Do you know what makes it ring? It has a little clapper inside which makes ringing sounds as it bounces against the sides. Our message comes from inside as well. It's our love for Jesus in our hearts which makes Christmas a special time of the year.

We are going to try an experiment with our bells. Hold the bell in your hand. Now try to ring it. It doesn't make a very clear sound, does it? When you let something touch your bell, it won't ring right. This is an important thing the jingle bell is telling us. We don't want anything to dull the Christmas message. It is easy to let parties and presents get in the way. We often wonder how many presents we will get or whether we will get the toys we have been asking for. We need to remember that we give presents to each other because it is Jesus' birthday. We have parties because it is a happy time of the year. The real meaning of Christmas is Jesus coming to earth as a baby. If presents and parties become so important that we forget the true meaning of Christmas, then we no longer have a clear message to ring.

Take your jingle bell home and let it remind you this whole Christmas season of what Christmas is really about.

15.

WHY SING?

OBJECT: A new song which is fun to sing. This may be made more interesting if an unusual instrument (violin, banjo, flute) is used to introduce the song.

LESSON: Singing is an important part of worship.

TEXT: "Sing a new song to the Lord; sing his praises, all the world!" (Isa. 42:10a).

OUTLINE

Introduce object: The object I have for you today is a violin with a new song.
1. We sing because it makes us happy.
2. We sing because it is a way of worshiping God together.
3. We sing to praise and thank God.
Conclusion: Singing is important for living a joyful Christian life.

The object I have for you today is a violin with a new song. Listen to it first and then we will sing along. We'll sing it until you know it well enough to really enjoy it. (Consult a book of songs for children, available at most Christian bookstores.)

How did you feel when you sang our new song? I could tell from your faces that you were happy. Our text tells us to "sing a new song to the Lord." One of the reasons we do this is because it makes us happy. Do you ever go around the house humming? I like to hum because it makes me feel so good. I enjoy singing new—and old—songs in church.

Another reason we sing today is that when we all sing a song together, we all worship together. It sounds wonderful when all of our voices blend in song. We can sing louder and have more fun when we sing together.

We also sing because it is a way to praise God. With some songs we are thanking God while we are singing. It is important to think about the *words* of the song when we are singing it. Then the song has special meaning for us. I especially enjoy the new songs which take the words of the Bible and put them to music. What a beautiful way to praise God!

We'll sing this song again just before we leave so we can remember it and go home singing it. Remember also that singing is a part of worship. Singing is important in living a joyful Christian life.

16.

NO LINK IS TOO SMALL

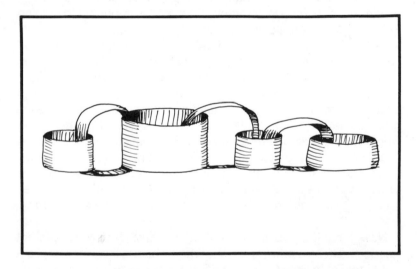

OBJECT: A paper chain with links of different sizes, different colors, and different textures.

LESSON: God needs all ages, sizes, and types of people in his kingdom. All have important jobs to do.

TEXT: "So they asked him, 'What can we do in order to do what God wants us to do?'" (John 6:28).

OUTLINE

Introduce object: What is different about this chain?
1. Nobody is the wrong age, size, color, or kind of person to be important in God's kingdom.
2. We all need to do our job or the chain will be broken.
3. We must all support each other.
Conclusion: Would you want to be the one to let go?

Do you like this chain? It's not an ordinary chain. What is different about it? That's right. The links are of different sizes. They are also different colors and kinds of paper. All of the links, however, have one thing in common. Each one is important in holding the chain together. No link can say, "I'm too small."

Yes, no person in God's kingdom is too small, too big, too young, too old, too thin, too fat, too black, too white, too sick, or too busy. Each is important in his own way for what he can do for God.

Every person has a job to do—even if it is just to be there to encourage the people who are leading. We must all support each other just as each link in this chain supports all of the others. The whole chain would be broken if just one link let go. Every one of us is dependent on the help and encouragement of those around us. A smile or a thank you can be as important as giving special music or delivering a speech. Helping our parents and teachers makes their job easier and more enjoyable. Any size or shape link can be a friend.

Now, what if this one little link here should decide he was not needed? (Break a small link.) The whole chain is broken. It will be a great deal of trouble to fix it again. Boys and girls, don't ever think you are not important in God's kingdom. Would you want to be the one to let go?

17.

THE STAR OF CHRISTMAS

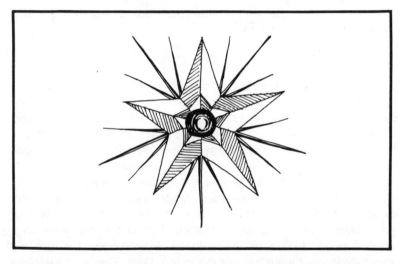

OBJECT: A star (a drawing, a cut-out, or a lighted Christmas ornament).

LESSON: What was the star? What guiding light do you follow in your life?

TEXT: " 'Where is the baby born to be the king of the Jews? We saw his star when it came up in the east, and we have come to worship him.' . . . And so they left, and on their way they saw the same star they had seen in the East. When they saw it, how happy they were, what joy was theirs! It went ahead of them until it stopped over the place where the child was" (Matt. 2:2, 9-10).

OUTLINE

Introduce object: This star represents the Christmas star.
1. What was the Christmas star? What is the guiding light in our lives?
2. What kind of search did the wise men have? Seeking Jesus is not always easy.

Conclusion: May you find Jesus' love shining brightly like a star in your lives this Christmas.

This star represents the Christmas star. There are many opinions about what the star the wise men saw in the east really was. Some people think it was a special star which God created to lead the wise men to the baby Jesus, and that it disappeared when it had done this. Others think that it was a bright light like a super nova or a comet.

In Bible times people called all of the small lights in the night sky *stars*. Since only the wise men report seeing the star, many people believe that the star in the east was a special crossing of three planets in the house of Pisces. This is a name given to a special group of stars, or constellation, which people thought told about things that were happening to the Jews. This would explain why the wise men went to Jerusalem to ask where the baby born to be king of the Jews might be found.

This star can also stand for the leading of God's spirit in our lives, as the star led the wise men. This guidance might be a strong leading in our lives, or it might be a small tugging on our hearts which we must carefully follow.

What kind of search did the wise men have? It was a long one. They traveled in the days when there were no airplanes or trains or cars. They may have had camels to travel on, or they may have come on foot. They had to stop often to eat and to rest. But they didn't give up. And after they left Jerusalem, they saw the star again and were led to where Jesus was. What does this mean for us? Seeking Jesus is not always easy, but the rewards are great.

May you find Jesus' love shining brightly like a star in your lives this Christmas.

18.

NEW YEAR'S RESOLUTION

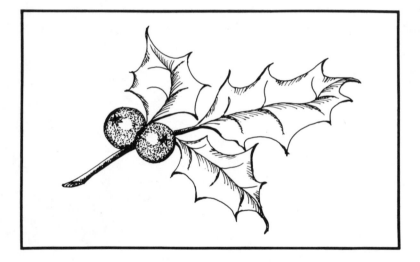

OBJECT: Holly.

LESSON: Make a New Year's resolution to let God help you every day to be attractive, not irritable.

TEXT: "The Lord's unfailing love and mercy still continue, fresh as the morning, as sure as the sunrise" (Lam. 3:22, 23).

OUTLINE

Introduce object: I have some interesting things to tell you about this plant.
1. The significance of holly in history.
    A. Ancient people used holly to drive away evil spirits.
    B. To the early church holly represented Jesus' sacrifice.
2. The significance of holly for you as a New Year's resolution.
    A. It is beautiful but irritating.
    B. Resolve with God's help to be attractive but not irritable or irritating.
Conclusion: You must rely on God's help every day.

I have something interesting to tell you about this plant. Do you know what it is called? That's right, holly. We often see it around during the Christmas season because of its red and green color. There are over 150 different kinds of holly. The plants range from small bushes to tall trees. There are male and female holly trees. Both have small flowers, but only the female trees have berries. Some holly are evergreen—they keep their leaves all winter. Others lose their leaves in the fall. American Holly is the state tree of Delaware. Most holly has thorns or prickly leaves. You wouldn't want to grab a bunch of this holly with your bare hands!

Holly has been significant to people for a long time. Ancient people thought it was useful to poke at evil spirits and scare them away. People in the early Christian church were more concerned with loving Jesus than with scaring evil spirits. Holly reminded them of Jesus death for them. The pricklyness stands for the crown of thorns placed on Jesus' head. The red berries look like drops of Jesus' blood. The green color represents everlasting life.

We may not think of holly in this way, but it still can have meaning for us. It is a beautiful plant, but it is prickly to work with. It makes a lovely wreath, but you really hurt your hands when you make one. Can the holly say something to us for the new year? I think so. We do want to be attractive to others so that they can see the special love of Jesus through us. But we don't want to be prickly. We don't want to irritate or hurt others. We also don't want to be irritable or cranky. This is a big job. To do this we must rely on God's help every day.

19.
WISE MEN STILL SEEK HIM
(EPIPHANY)

OBJECT: A picture, statues, or other fairly accurate representation of the wise men.

LESSON: Who were the wise men?

TEXT: "Jesus was born in the town of Bethlehem in Judea, during the time when Herod was king. Soon afterward, some men who studied the stars came from the

East to Jerusalem. . . . They went into the house, and when they saw the child with his mother Mary, they knelt down and worshiped him (Matt. 2:1, 11a).

OUTLINE

Introduce object: What do you know about the wise men?
1. Epiphany is a special day to remember the wise men who came to visit Jesus as a young child.
2. Errors have occurred as people have retold the Bible story.
   A. Only the wise men saw the star.
   B. The wise men were men who studied the stars; they were not kings.
   C. The Bible doesn't tell us how many wise men there were.
3. The wise men prove that Jesus came not only for the Jews but for other people too.
Conclusion: Wise men still seek him.

What do you know about the wise men? Chances are a lot of you have heard some ideas that are not true. Many people think the wise men came to see the newborn baby Jesus in the manger. Actually, the trip probably took them about two years. They stopped in Jerusalem to ask Herod, the ruler of the Jews, where this new king of the Jews was. Herod called his scholars and asked them what the prophets wrote. They said that the Messiah was to be born in Bethlehem.

Herod sent the wise men to Bethlehem, but told them to come back to him and tell him all about the baby. When the wise men did not return (they were warned in a dream), Herod ordered all of the boys two years old and younger in Bethlehem and the neighboring towns to be killed. This tells us that Jesus was probably about two years old by that time. Fortunately, an angel told Joseph and Mary to go to Egypt, and they escaped Herod's terrible persecution.

Since the wise men did not come to the manger, we have a

special day to remember them. It is called *Epiphany* and it comes after Christmas.

Have you seen pictures of the shepherds watching the star? The Bible tells us that only the wise men saw the star. The shepherds saw the angels, whose bright light was the glory of God.

How many of you think that the wise men were kings? The Bible does not tell us that. We only know that they were men who studied the stars. At Christmas we often sing the song, "We Three Kings of Orient Are," but the Bible does not tell us how many wise men there were. We do know that they brought three different gifts.

Are the wise men important to the Christmas story? Yes, they tell us that Jesus came not only for the Jewish people but for others as well. The wise men were not Jews, but God led them to the baby.

What else can we learn from the wise men? We are reminded that we must still search to learn about Jesus as the wise men did long ago. You may see this saying on a bumper sticker or Christmas card: *Wise men still seek him!*

20.

WHAT IS YOUR REACTION TIME?

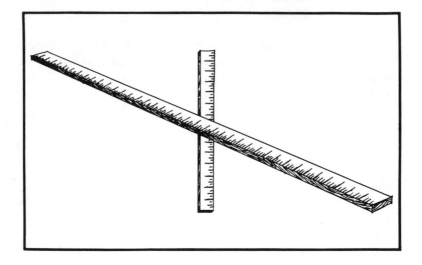

OBJECT: A yardstick.

LESSON: How fast do you react when someone needs help?

TEXT: ". . . remembering the words that the Lord Jesus him-self said, 'There is more happiness in giving than in receiving'" (Acts 20:35b).

OUTLINE

Introduce object: I will need several volunteers today.
1. Will you help? Excuses for not helping.
2. How soon will you help? Do you need to think about it first?
Conclusion: What is your reaction time for helping others?

I will need several volunteers today. (Hold yardstick with largest measurement on top.) I want to check your reaction time, to see how fast you can catch this yardstick through your thumb and forefinger. When you see me let go of the yardstick, catch it yourself. The distance from the beginning of the yardstick and the place where you catch it is your reaction time. Let's see who can catch it at the lowest number. (Have each child sit down as he is finished.)

When I first asked for volunteers, not everybody wanted to help. Suppose I walked up here with my arms full and started dropping things. Would you come up here and help me? It is important to be willing to help. Don't let yourself make excuses like: "Somebody else will do it if I just sit here"; "somebody else can do it much better than I can"; "it's some other person's job to do that"; or "they don't need me"! Everybody needs some help sometime. Somebody certainly will need you.

We were testing your reaction time for catching the yardstick. We learned that different people have different reaction times. First your eye has to see that I have let go of the stick. It sends a message to your brain, which tells your hand to catch the stick. When you see a person in trouble, your eye sends a message to your brain. You think about it and then decide if you will help.

How soon will you respond if someone needs help? Do you have to sit and think about it for awhile? Do you argue with yourself and make excuses? If you wait long enough, the problem the person needed help with may be worse.

Are you aware of people around you who need help? Do you go over to a child who is crying? Do you help when something is spilled? Do you lend a hand when someone has a lot of work to do? Will you listen to a person's problems and try to solve them?

What is your reaction time for helping others?

21.

A POPPED CHRISTIAN

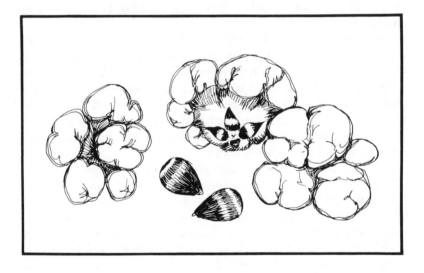

OBJECT: A large bag of unpopped popcorn and a bag of popped corn.

LESSON: Live the Christian life to its fullest by developing your God-given potential.

TEXT: "For the full content of divine nature lives in Christ, in his humanity, and you have been given full life in union with him" (Col. 2:9-10a).

OUTLINE

Introduce object: Popcorn is different from regular corn because it has moisture inside of a very hard shell. This moisture when heated turns to steam. The steam builds up until the shell bursts open into the white blossom we know so well.

1. The nature of unpopped corn
   A. It has moisture inside the hard shell.
   B. The Christian has the love for Jesus inside.
2. The process of popping
   A. Heat makes steam which expands and pops the shell.
   B. The freedom of Jesus' love for us warms us to pop into creative, joyful Christians.
3. The nature of popcorn
   A. Each blossom is unique.
   B. Each Christian is different and special.

Conclusion: The neatest thing about popcorn is watching it pop. It is even more delightful to see you become the special Christian Jesus wants you to be.

Today I brought something we all know about and enjoy—popcorn. Popcorn is different from regular corn because it has moisture inside of a very hard shell. This moisture, when heated, turns to steam. The steam builds up until the shell bursts open into the white blossom we know so well. It is delicious to eat. You can hardly tell it is a vegetable!

Christians are special on the inside also. They have something different that sets them apart from others. Christians have love for Jesus.

If all Christians have love for Jesus inside of them, why are they not all living joyful lives? Well, why is that popcorn hard and dry while this popcorn is white and fluffy and looks delicious? The fluffy popcorn had to be popped. Just *being* popcorn was not enough. It had to be heated until enough moisture was changed to steam to make the shell pop. Christians are warmed by Jesus' love for them until they also pop into creative, joyful people. As

Jesus' love grows in them they become more loving, caring, and happy people.

Have you ever taken a close look at your popped popcorn? Do it the next time you have some and you will notice that each blossom is different. They look similar from a distance but when you examine them closely you will find that each one has popped in a slightly different way. Christians, too, are all alike in Christ, but yet each one is unique, special, different. Each Christian has his own gifts, special interests, and talents. Each has his own contribution to give.

It is not pleasant to see tight, unpopped Christians. The neatest thing about popcorn is watching it pop. It is even more delightful to see *you* become the special Christian Jesus wants you to be.

22.

COLORED POPCORN

OBJECT: Colored popcorn (available in most well-stocked supermarkets but might be located in the gourmet section). Pop some of it and put it in a plastic bag. Put the remainder of unpopped corn in a clear container.

LESSON: God has made people different.

TEXT: "So there is no difference between Jews and Gentiles, between slaves and free men, between men and

women; you are all one in union with Christ Jesus"
(Gal. 3:28).

OUTLINE

Introduce object: How many of you have ever seen colored popcorn?
1. All kernels are white when they pop.
2. Color makes popcorn more interesting.
Conclusion: I am glad that God has made different colors in his
world.

How many of you have ever seen colored popcorn? It comes
this way in the store—blue, yellow, orange, red, and green kernels
of corn. Do you suppose the red ones pop into red-colored popcorn blossoms, the green ones into green blossoms, the blue into
blue blossoms? Would you like to find out? (Keep popped corn out
of sight until this point.) Look at this! All of the colors are the same
on the inside. They all popped white.

What about black people? Are they different inside? How about
brown or red people? Are they different on the inside since they
are so different on the outside? No? Then what about the yellow
people? Are they different? Not them either? Does that mean that
God loves us all and has made us all in his image? Do you think
we all look alike to him?

When you take a closer look at this bag of popped corn, you can
see that there are still little bits of the colored shell sticking to the
popcorn. It really is quite pretty to see the different colors clinging
to the white popcorn. That is why they make different colored
popcorn. It is more expensive to buy but it is more interesting than
regular popcorn. I wonder why God made people different colors.
He could have made everyone alike. Do you think the world is
more interesting with different kinds and colors of people in it? I
do. I am glad that God has made different colors in his world.

23.

FELLOWSHIP

OBJECT: A candle in a small holder and a glass container
which will fit over the burning candle and holder, cutting off the oxygen supply.

LESSON: Fellowship, like oxygen, is invisible but important. It is
something we give to each other.

TEXT: "Your life in Christ makes you strong, and his love
comforts you. The Spirit has brought you into fellow-

ship with one another; and you have kindness and compassion for one another" (Phil. 2:1).

OUTLINE

Introduce object: The Bible tells us to let our light shine, so I am going to light my candle.
1. The need for oxygen; the need for fellowship (indispensable)
2. The nature of oxygen; the nature of fellowship (invisible)
Conclusion: You need other Christians and they need you. This is something very important we give to each other.

The Bible tells us to let our light shine, so I am going to light my candle. But I don't want anything to happen to my brightly burning flame, so I am going to cover it carefully. After all, a puff of wind might come along and blow it out. I certainly wouldn't want *that* to happen! Now look at how safely it's shining. See—this candle doesn't need anything or anybody else to make it burn! But wait a minute! My flame went out. What happened? Did you blow it out? Well, I certainly didn't blow it out!

Who can tell us why my candle couldn't burn all by itself under the glass? Yes, a candle needs oxygen to burn. My flame burned up the oxygen and couldn't get any more because it was covered.

That oxygen in the air certainly is important. Just as the candle cannot burn when it is separated from the oxygen, the Christian cannot shine when he is separated from the fellowship of other Christians. "Fellowship" means sharing, being kind, caring for and about others, and loving the same Jesus together. Christians need fellowship to burn, to shine, to live happy lives. We can't stay by ourselves and still expect to be the kind of Christians the Bible talks about. That is not the way God made us.

We cannot see oxygen. It is invisible. But we know there is oxygen in this room because the candle did burn until we cut off its oxygen supply. And we all need oxygen to breathe. So even though we can't see the oxygen, we know it's here. In the same way, we cannot see fellowship, but when we see a group of Christians singing together and enjoying it, we know that fellowship is there. When we see a group of Christians talking and laughing and hugging each other, we know that fellowship is there. When we see someone with a smile on his face because he has done something for someone else, we know that fellowship is there.

You need other Christians and they need you. This is something very important we give to each other.

24.

GOD IS ETERNAL

OBJECT: A thick rope or clothesline long enough to stretch from one window or door, across the room, and out another window or door without either end being seen. Set this up before the audience enters.

LESSON: God is eternal. We meet him here but go on with him into eternity.

TEXT: "Before you created the hills or brought the world into being, you were eternally God, and will be God forever" (Ps. 90:2).

OUTLINE

Introduce object: You cannot see the beginning or ending of this rope. I brought it here today to help explain what is meant by our Bible verse—that God is eternal.

1. God is eternal—he existed before the world and will exist forever.
2. When we believe in God we go on with him into eternity.

Conclusion: How wonderful to think that our lives will not end but go on into eternity with him.

You cannot see the beginning or ending of this rope. I brought it here today to help explain what is meant by our Bible verse—that God is eternal. God existed before he created our world with its hills and trees and rivers. He existed before everyone and everything. He has always existed. Just as there seems to be no beginning to this rope, so there *is* no beginning to God. (Shake rope and watch until the movement stops.) There is also no ending to God. He will go on and on forever. (Shake rope again.) God is eternal.

We know when a person begins. He is born on a certain date—perhaps here (pick up rope). He lives for a length of time and then dies (move along rope for a distance and drop it). Or perhaps she is born here (pick up rope in a different place), lives a longer time, and dies here (move a longer distance along the rope in the same direction and drop it). But God is eternal. The Bible says that "God loved the world so much that he gave his only Son, so that everyone who believes in him may not die but have eternal life," John 3:16.

Yes, when we believe in God we go on with him into eternity. We are born at a certain time and our bodies die at a certain time—but dying is not an ending, a dropping of the rope. It is a time when we leave behind our bodies and continue to be with God forever. How wonderful to think that our lives will not end but go on into eternity with him.

25.

VALENTINE'S DAY

OBJECT: A plain box containing a fancy box with candy inside.

LESSON: If you have something special in your life, let it be seen from the outside.

TEXT: "And now I give you a new commandment: love one another. As I have loved you, so you must love one another. If you have love for one another, then everyone will know that you are my disciples" (John 13:34–35).

OUTLINE

Introduce object: What do you think is in this box?
1. You would choose for yourself the more attractive box.
2. The way to be more attractive is to be more loving.
Conclusion: Let every day be Valentine's day.

What do you think is in this box (the plain outside box)? It could be empty. Perhaps it holds a trick snake that will jump out when I open it. Or, it may be just a box of junk I've had sitting around the house. You really can't tell anything from looking at the outside of this plain box. We'll have to open it and find out what's inside. (Open box.) Look at this fancy box on the inside! It is shaped like a heart. Have you ever seen a box like this one before? Do you think you know what is in it?

You can never tell for sure by looking only at the outside of something. It is not good to judge people by their outside appearance, but other people *do* make decisions about us by the way we look and act. Just think for a minute. If you could choose for yourself one of the boxes, which one would you choose? It would be smart to look inside first, but you cannot see what is in this fancy box from where you are sitting. If you had no idea what was in either box, you would probably choose the fancy box. For the same reason, people are naturally drawn to a person with an attractive outlook and personality. Let's open this fancy box and see what is in it. Yum, candy.

How can you look attractive from the outside? The most important thing to have is love. Valentine's Day is a day we are supposed to show our love for those around us. We give cards and candy and hugs. When we act more loving, we feel better. When we feel happier, we are more attractive. Jesus tells us to "love one another." We need to show this love every day. Let every day be Valentine's Day.

26.

VISIBLE AND INVISIBLE BRUISES

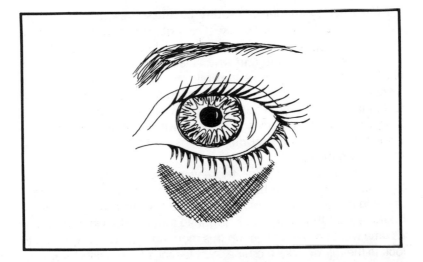

OBJECT: A bad bruise (I used a lovely large black eye which I received roller skating with the children. If no real bruises are available, one can be applied with makeup).

LESSON: Set a wrong straight before it becomes worse.

TEXT: "'I, the Lord, command you to do what is just and right'" (Jer. 22:3a).

OUTLINE

Introduce object: Describe how the bruise was received.

1. The first impact or act of unkindness hurts.
2. As time passes the injured blood vessels bleed into the skin. An unkindness grows worse as a person thinks it over.
3. Bruises must be left to fade. Acts of unkindness may be righted.

Conclusion: If you have done something to hurt another person, don't let any more time go by. Don't let the hurt get worse. Make it right today!

I am wearing sunglasses today because the object I brought with me is under them. I'll take them off, but be prepared for a shock. I went roller skating yesterday and met up with the floor.

I must admit that it *did* hurt when I fell. In fact, I was knocked out briefly. I'll never forget how that felt. We all know what it's like to have our feelings hurt, too. When you do or say something unkind to someone, it hurts. That expression is not true: "Sticks and stones will break my bones but names will never hurt me." Calling someone names *will* hurt our feelings. In fact, it can hurt *more* than a slap or a push.

Yesterday, when I first fell, there was only a red mark where I hit the floor. However, an hour or two later the blood vessels that I broke in the fall began to bleed under the skin and my eye turned a bright red. As the blood set, it began to turn purple. I looked worse as time went on. When I got up this morning I could hardly stand to look in the mirror. Like a bruise, hurt feelings from unkind words or actions grow worse as a person thinks about them. The more you remember them, the worse they feel.

Nothing will help this bruise but time. In a couple of weeks it will fade to an ugly yellow and then it will go away. I may always have a little scar where I hit the floor. Something can, however, be done about unkindnesses we have done to others. If we are fast enough and sincere enough, often a simple "I'm sorry" will take care of it.

Sometimes we need to do something kind to take away the unkindness. Ask the person who has been hurt, "What can I do to make it right again?"

If you have done something to hurt another person, don't let any more time go by. Don't let the hurt get worse. Make it right today!

27.

THE TONGUE

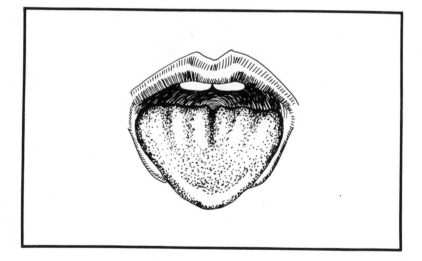

OBJECT: A drawing of a tongue or a cow's tongue from a meat market. Five cards with the texts printed on them.

LESSON: The control of the tongue is a difficult but important task.

TEXTS: Proverbs 17:27–28; 12:16; 16:23; 18:20–26.

OUTLINE

Introduce object: Can you tell what is in this drawing? It is something we all brought with us today. I am using mine right now.
1. The art of keeping silent (Prov. 17:27-28) even when provoked (Prov. 12:16).
2. The importance of thinking before speaking (Prov. 16:23).
3. The responsibility connected with speaking (Prov. 18:20, 21).
Conclusion: Thank God you have a tongue—but use it wisely (Prov. 16:24)!

Can you tell what is in this drawing? It is something we all brought with us today. I am using mine right now. Yes, it is a tongue. The tongue is a strange-looking little thing, isn't it? It is a muscle which is attached to the floor of the mouth. It is necessary for eating and pronouncing many sounds. Try saying the word "lollipop" without using your tongue.

Because we need our tongues for speaking, our tongues can get us into trouble. This kind of trouble has been going on for as long as people have been using their tongues. The Book of Proverbs—wise sayings written before Jesus lived on earth—contains many references to speaking. Let's see how it tells us to use our tongue.

We are given some very good advice about keeping silent. Silence is an art to be developed. "Someone who is sure of himself does not talk all the time. People who stay calm have real insight. After all, even a fool may be thought wise and intelligent if he stays quiet and keeps his mouth shut." (Hold up card containing Prov. 17:27-28.) It is even more difficult to keep still when someone says something to provoke us. But we are told: "When a fool is annoyed, he quickly lets it be known. Smart people will ignore an insult." (Hold up card with Prov. 12:16 written on it.)

It is neither possible nor desirable to *always* be silent, so we need to learn what to do when we speak. Can you guess what is the most important thing to do *before* you speak? Yes, think first! Proverbs tells us: "Intelligent people think before they speak; what they say is then more persuasive." (Hold up Prov. 16:23.)

You can pull the stinger from a bee sting, but that doesn't remove the poison; and you can take back words you have said but that doesn't take back their impact. Again Proverbs says: "You will have to live with the consequences of everything you say. What you say can preserve life or destroy it: so you must accept the consequences of your words." (Hold up Prov. 18:20, 21.)

Thank God you have a tongue—but use it wisely! "Kind words are like honey—sweet to the taste and good for your health." (Hold up Prov. 16:24.)

28.
A TUNEFUL LIFE

OBJECT: A set of 18-ounce glasses with increasing amounts of water in them, arranged so they will play a scale. Choose a song for demonstration which can be played with the notes you have. Use a spoon or other metal object to strike the glasses.

LESSON: Arrange your priorities so you can live a tuneful life.

TEXT: "Righteous men will be happy, and things will go well for them. They will get to enjoy what they have worked for" (Isa. 3:10).

OUTLINE

Introduce object: Did you know that when you put water into a glass you can change its tune?
1. Decide which glasses have highest and lowest notes. Decide which activities in your life are most and least important.
2. Arrange the glasses (your activities) in order.
3. Now you are able to play a tune (live a tuneful life).
Conclusion: Decide today what things are most important in your life.

Did you know that when you put water into a glass you can change its tune? (Demonstrate, striking a glass only half filled, and striking it again when it is filled to the top.) I have some more glasses which all play different notes (have the glasses on a table in random order). I can't do much with them this way, so I am going to arrange them in order. (Arrange them so that glasses are in an ascending scale, the lowest notes to the highest representing the most important activities to the least in left to right reading order for those facing you.)

We all have many different activities. We go to school; we play; we clean our room; we watch TV; we do our homework; we help our mother. . . . Some of these things are more important than others. We would get into trouble if we played instead of doing our homework. We wouldn't get our allowance if we watched TV instead of cleaning our rooms. We would be unhappy if we spent so much time doing things that really didn't matter and ran out of time to do the things we know God wants us to do.

In fact, a good way to decide what is most important is to ask ourselves what God would want us to do first. That way we can place the things that have the highest value first, just like I put the glasses with the highest notes first. It is important to remember that you need to arrange your time so that these things do get done before other, less important things.

Now that we have the glasses and our lives in order, we are ready to play a tune. (Play song.) Your life can also be tuneful and happy.

Decide today what things are most important in your life.

29.

DO YOU BELIEVE?

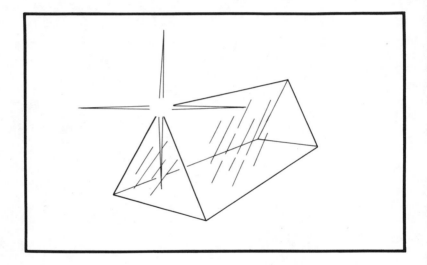

OBJECT: A prism and a beam of light from a projector to refract in the prism.

LESSON: Faith is believing in what we cannot see.

TEXT: "To have faith is to be sure of the things we hope for, to be certain of the things we cannot see" (Heb. 11:1).

OUTLINE

Introduce object: Do you believe that there are colors in this beam of light?

1. Faith is believing—as you believe what I say about the colors in a beam of light.
2. Faith is reflected in the lives of Christians as the beam of light is refracted by the prism.
3. Faith is finding more to life than meets the eye just as there are more colors to the rainbow than you can see.

Conclusion: It is all there for the believing—just have faith.

Do you believe that there are colors in this beam of light? It looks very white, but watch what happens when it is bent by this little triangular piece of glass we call a *prism.* There, up on the wall you can see a rainbow. If you look carefully enough, you can see several colors.

Did you believe me when I said that there are colors in a beam of light? Some of you know that I am honest, and you trust what I say. Do you believe God when he says in the Bible that he loves you—enough to even send his son to die for you? When you believe this without actually seeing it, this is called *faith.*

You did believe me once you saw the colors in the beam of light bent by the prism and reflected on the wall. You can learn about God's love by seeing it reflected in other people. Their lives show you what faith in God has done for them. Then you realize it can bring you the same happiness.

There are more colors in this rainbow than we can see. There is "infrared" past the red we see and "ultraviolet" past the purple. Our eyes cannot see them. Faith, too, is finding more to life than meets the eye. Through faith we can find deeper meaning to life than we ever dreamed was there. We can find more warmth and riches in God's love than we can possibly imagine. It is all there for the believing—just have faith.

30.

A HOLLOW LOAF
(EASTER)

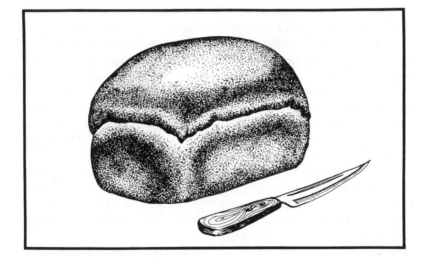

OBJECT: A hollow loaf of bread. (To prepare, select a loaf of
hard-crusted bread, unsliced. Cut a "trap door" in the
bottom, large enough for your hand. Gently pull out
the trap door and remove the soft bread from the
center of the loaf. Replace the trap door and glue in
place or hold with several toothpicks. During the demonstration use a very sharp knife and a sawing motion

to cut the bread, and the loaf will not collapse or appear to be empty while being cut.)

LESSON: This object demonstrates the emotions felt when people discovered the empty tomb.

TEXT: "They found the stone rolled away from the entrance to the tomb, so they went in; but they did not find the body of the Lord Jesus" (Luke 24:2-3).

OUTLINE

Introduce object: Doesn't this loaf of bread look good?

1. You are surprised at the empty loaf. They were surprised at the empty tomb.
2. You are curious about how a loaf of bread can be empty. They were curious about what happened to Jesus.
3. You are amazed that an empty loaf can actually be cut and not appear to be empty. They were amazed that Jesus had risen as he said he would.

Conclusion: If you can imagine yourself at the empty tomb, you can know something of how they felt. Jesus died for them and he died for us. How much he loves us.

Doesn't this loaf of bread look good? Have you ever had this kind of bread before? Do you know what it tastes like? I brought a knife with me so that I can cut the loaf. (Cut through center, open, and hold so all can see the loaf is empty.) What? You say the loaf is empty? How could that be!

Today is Easter when we remember that Jesus rose from the grave. When the women came to the grave to take care of Jesus' body, what did they see? That's right. It was empty. You were surprised to find this loaf of bread empty. Think how much more surprised the women were to find the tomb empty. How would you have felt if you were there?

I heard some of you say, "How did the bread get empty?" You

had good reason to be curious about this loaf of bread. Think again of the empty tomb. Would you wonder where Jesus was and what happened to him when you found him gone from his grave?

I cut a hole in the bottom of this loaf of bread and took out all of the inside part. Then I glued the bottom back together. Now you know why the loaf of bread was empty. Do you know why the tomb was empty? Yes, Jesus had risen just like he said he would.

It was too wonderful for the women to believe. They were amazed that Jesus had risen. That meant that he had *let* himself die, even though he had the power to get off the cross anytime he wanted to. You were amazed that an empty loaf of bread could have appeared to be whole. Think how much more amazed the people were that Jesus had actually risen.

If you can imagine yourself at the empty tomb, you can know something of how the women felt. Jesus died for them and he died for us. How much he loves us!

31.

DON'T BLOW YOUR TOP

OBJECT: A test tube (or coke bottle) with a cork stopper; vinegar; and baking soda. Fill test tube or bottle about a quarter of the way or less with vinegar. Add ½ to 1 teaspoon of baking soda. Cover test tube or bottle quickly but not too tightly with cork stopper. Keep test tube in upright position over a bowl which will catch any mixture which bubbles out. Keep a towel handy.

As the chemicals react, they will build up pressure which will pop the cork. Practice this over a big sink.

LESSON: A gentle response in conversation keeps anger from erupting.

TEXT: "A gentle answer quiets anger, but a harsh one stirs it up" (Prov. 15:1).

OUTLINE

Introduce object: Pretend the liquid is a question and the white powder is an irritable answer. (Since these chemicals are easily available in the home, it may not be wise to tell young children what they are.)

1. Watch your conversation so that it will not irritate others.
2. Give a gentle reply when someone says something that irritates you.

Conclusion: Nobody said it would be easy, but with God's help you can do it.

I need a volunteer to help me with an experiment (choose an older child who will be able to put the cork in quickly). I want you to pretend that the liquid in this test tube is a question. There are polite questions and there are questions which make you feel irritable. Sometimes when your mother asks, "Did you clean your room yet?" you feel like giving a harsh answer. Let's pretend also that the white powder in this spoon is an answer. There are gentle, kind answers to even irritable questions. There are also unkind answers.

For this experiment we have an irritating question and a harsh answer. Do you know what happens when you put them together? Would you like to find out? Get ready, volunteer, to put the cork in quickly but not too tightly. Look! This question and answer caused such a reaction that the person blew his top.

This happens quite a bit, doesn't it? But it doesn't need to happen to us. You can control your conversation so that it doesn't irritate others. You have to work at it, though. It doesn't always come easy. Prayer will help you learn to be careful what you say.

But what happens when someone else says something unkind to us first? We don't need to blow our tops, even though that is the natural reaction. God will, if we trust him, give us the patience to reply quietly and politely. Our text says: "A gentle answer quiets anger, but a harsh one stirs it up." Try a quiet answer. Nobody said it would be easy, but with God's help you *can* do it.

32.

SO THAT'S WHAT YOU ARE!

OBJECT: A T-shirt or a sweatshirt which is labeled "Christian," preferably with an arrow (as in picture).

LESSON: How would you act if you really wore a sign that told everybody you are a Christian?

TEXT: "It was at Antioch that the believers were first called Christians" (Acts 11:26b).

OUTLINE

Introduce object: There are many clever T-shirts available. How do you like the one I am wearing?

1. If we had shirts that said "Christian," would you wear one?
2. If you wore one, how would you act?
3. How can you show you are a Christian without a shirt?

Conclusion: This week, pretend you are wearing a T-shirt that says "Christian." How will you act?

There are many clever T-shirts available. How do you like the one I am wearing? (This is especially effective if the shirt is hidden under a choir robe until this point.)

Let's suppose that I have a big pile of T-shirts like this one in various sizes and that I am giving them out to anyone who wants to wear one. Would *you* want to wear one? Think about that for a minute. It would mean everyone would know that you go to church, that you are a follower of Christ. It would take courage to wear one of the shirts.

If you decided to wear a shirt that tells everyone you are a Christian, how would you act? People would expect certain things of you. A follower of Christ tries to be like him. That means you need to be kind and honest and forgiving and many other things that are not always easy to be. That could be a lot of hard work.

Perhaps you *are* doing this without a shirt telling people who you are. People who know you already know that you go to church. Are you already acting and living like someone who is a follower of Christ? You don't need a shirt to do this. All you need is a prayer and determination.

Let's conduct an experiment. I am going to give out imaginary T-shirts. I want you to "wear" them and to think about what it means to have everyone who looks at you know what you are. This week, pretend you are wearing a T-shirt that says "Christian." How will *you* act?

33.

LOVE YOUR ENEMIES

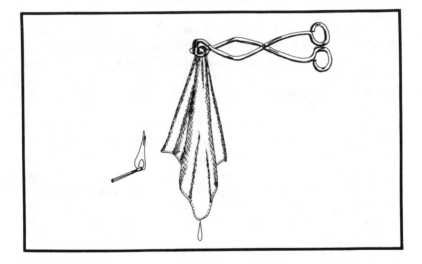

OBJECT: A paper napkin soaked in a solution of half water and half alcohol. Hold the napkin with tongs. When it is set on fire, the alcohol will burn quickly, leaving the napkin intact.

LESSON: It seems impossible to love your enemies. The trick to it is that we use Jesus' love.

TEXT: "But I tell you who hear me: Love your enemies, do good to those who hate you, bless those who curse you, and pray for those who mistreat you" (Luke 6:27, 28).

OUTLINE

Introduce object: Do you think I can burn this wet paper napkin?
1. It doesn't seem possible to burn a wet paper napkin. It doesn't seem possible to love our enemies.
2. What we are really burning is the alcohol. What we are really loving with is the love of Jesus.
3. The alcohol burns out. Jesus' love is never ending.
Conclusion: Do you have the courage to use that powerful kind of love?

Do you think I can burn this wet paper napkin? No? We all know that a plain paper napkin burns quickly and easily. We also know that something that is wet does not burn well. I'm going to try anyway. (Demonstrate.) Yes, it did burn. It didn't seem possible that it would. But look, the napkin isn't damaged. How could that be? You saw it burn.

There is something else that seems impossible. The Bible tells us to love our enemies. An enemy is someone who tries to hurt us either with words or actions. We are even told to pray for those who are mean to us. How can we do that? It is easy to love people who are nice to us and like us.

Do you think you could love somebody who hates you and says mean things to you—somebody who hits you? Yes, you can, but there is a trick to it. Our own love isn't strong enough. We have to use Jesus' love. What was really burning when I burned the napkin was the alcohol that I soaked it in. Alcohol burns at a lower temperature than the napkin, so it was able to burn without setting the napkin on fire. Jesus has a lower loving temperature than we do. He can love where we cannot.

If we ask Jesus for his love, he will give us enough to love our enemies. The best part of it is that, even though the alcohol burns out, Jesus' love will never run out. There is more than enough for everybody and every need.

Do you have the courage to use that powerful kind of love?

34.

GOD'S CREATION

OBJECT: Bird's nest (or any interesting object of nature—a flower, a weed, a feather). Use this lesson when you need an object quickly or on a nature walk.

LESSON: God has created this earth for us to enjoy and to show us of His great love for us.

TEXT: "As for you, even the hairs of your head have all been counted" (Matt. 10:30).

OUTLINE

Introduce object: Have you ever looked closely and wondered at how well-made a bird's nest is?
1. God wants you to "wonder about" His creation.
2. God is showing you how much He also cares for you.
Conclusion: Let the little things in God's creation remind us of His greatness and His love for us.

How many times have you stopped to notice all of the marvelous little things in God's creation? Have you ever looked closely and wondered at how well-made a bird's nest is? Look at this nest that was found fallen from a tree. The pieces of grass and twigs have been carefully woven into a sturdy growing place for busy little birds. The nest is lined with something soft so the baby birds will be comfortable. It is so small that I can barely fit my hand into it. Isn't it wonderful?

I have used the words *wonder* and *wonderful* because they are the best ones to describe how great God's creation is and how it makes us feel. To wonder means to admire, to delight in, to marvel at something beautiful. It is the feeling that you get when you say, "Isn't that *wonderful!*" God gave you His creation so that you could wonder about it. He wants you to take notice of the small, beautifully-formed things He has made. In wondering about them you cannot help feeling a sense of awe at the greatness of our God who has made them. Take time to notice the small objects in nature. Enjoy them!

God not only *made* the little things of nature, He cares for them. If He cares for them, how much more must He care for us! Our text tells us that even the hairs of our head are counted. If God knows that much about us, think of how concerned He is with how we think, how we act, and what we say. How wonderful that our great God cares for every detail in our lives.

Let the little things in God's creation remind us of His greatness and His love for us.

35.

FOUNDATIONS

OBJECT: History of the changes of the building you are in, if it is suitable. Otherwise use pictures or diagrams of another, more appropriate one.

LESSON: People change, as do buildings, but the basic foundation, faith in Jesus, remains the same.

TEXT: "But the solid foundation that God has laid cannot be shaken; and on it are written these words: 'The Lord knows those who are his' and 'whoever says that he belongs to the Lord must turn away from wrongdoing'" (II Tim. 2:19).

OUTLINE

Introduce object: Give the history of the building changes.
1. The building has experienced change. People change.
2. The basic structure is unaltered. Our faith in Jesus remains the same.
3. The building rests on a solid foundation. Jesus is our solid foundation.
Conclusion: We may change, but *he* won't!

This church you are sitting in today is over 150 years old. It used to have kerosene lamps hanging from the ceiling and doors on the pews. Women brought foot warmers in the winter because there was no heat. Men were considered too hearty to need such a luxury. Later, electric lamps replaced the kerosene ones so that the women no longer needed to climb up the high ladders to clean and fill them. Stoves were put in the back of the church with long pipes running under the balconies to give warmth in the winter. Still later, the furnaces were moved downstairs. Recently the sanctuary was carpeted. There have been many changes in this old church, and there will be more.

People change as well. They grow up, grow out, grow old. . . . Their ideas change. People move away or make new friends. Hopefully they become wiser, more patient, and kinder.

The basic faith of Christians, however, remains the same. Just as the church is still used to hold the children of God, so too the Christian still has as his life's center a deep love for Jesus. Inside you are still you even when you grow up and look different.

This church has a solid stone foundation which is still strong after all of these years. We have a foundation which will always be firm. Jesus will never change. He will always love us. He will always be there for us. He will always help us. We may change, but *he* won't!

36.

MOTHER'S CONCERNS

(MOTHER'S DAY)

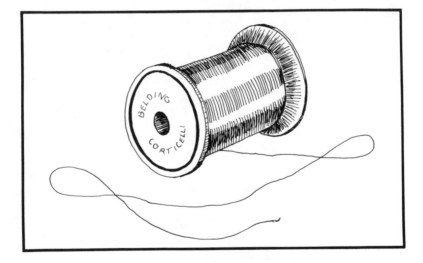

OBJECT: A spool of thread.

LESSON: Mothers must keep telling you to do or not to do things in order to help you develop good habits.

TEXT: " 'Assemble the people. I want them to hear what I have to say, so that they will learn to reverently obey me as long as they live and so that they will teach their children to obey me' " (Deut. 4:10b).

OUTLINE

Introduce object: Choose a volunteer to help demonstrate that thread is easy to break unless it is wrapped around them many times.

1. Good habits: Our mothers keep telling us to do things because the more we do them, the more likely we are to continue doing them.
2. Bad habits: Mothers must stop us from doing things we should not do.
3. God has given mothers a difficult responsibility.

Conclusion: This Mother's Day is a good time for you to decide to help your mother with this tough job!

I will need a volunteer. Do you think you are strong enough to break this thread? I'm going to wrap it around your wrists once or twice. Yes, that was easy to break. This time I am going to wrap it several times. I see you had to struggle to break the thread that time.

Hm, you look like a pretty good kid. Do you always do what your mother tells you to do? Each time she reminds you to do something and you obey her it is like wrapping this thread around your wrists again and again (wrap as you talk). Let's take an example. Every night your mother reminds you to say your prayers. The more you do this, the more likely you will be to remember to do this by yourself. Soon you have formed a good habit. Now try to break the thread. You seem to be having a little trouble. A few threads were easy to break but many of them really have you tied. You'll have to go back to your seat and I'll check with you in about an hour to see how you are doing. Your mother sees to it that you do the right thing many times because she wants you to have good habits.

Your mother also stops you from doing or saying the wrong things. She knows that bad habits are even easier to make and harder to break. The more you do something wrong the less it seems like the wrong thing to do. Have you ever lied to your mother about something you have done so that she would not punish you for it? Be careful! You know it is wrong, but the more you do it the easier it becomes. Soon she will not be able to trust you.

God has given your mother the task of helping you make good habits and avoid bad habits. That is quite a responsibility! Your mother has to talk a lot and punish a lot to do this. This Mother's Day is a good time for you to decide to help your mother with this tough job.

37.

WALK A MILE IN HIS MOCCASINS

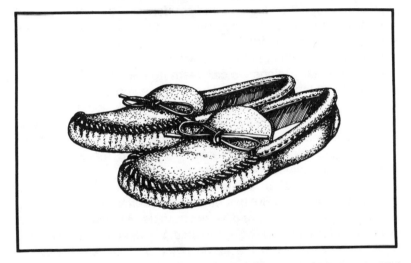

OBJECT: An Indian moccasin or a slipper designed in Indian style.

LESSON: To love your neighbor you must understand him. Understanding comes when you "walk a mile in his moccasins."

TEXT: "The second most important commandment is this: 'Love your neighbor as you love yourself'" (Mark 12:31a).

OUTLINE

Introduce object: North American Indians wore a special kind of shoe.

1. Who is your neighbor?
2. "Walk a mile in his moccasins" means to understand his problems.

Conclusion: Our neighbors are not just the people who live next to us on our street. God wants you to love all of the people he has created.

North American Indians wore a special kind of shoe. How many of you have ever had slippers that looked like this? Moccasins are popular because they are soft and comfortable. Indians designed moccasins to meet their needs and used the materials they had. They cut them from leather which they made from animal skins. With them an Indian could hunt quietly.

There are many things we can learn from Indians. The Indians have a saying that I especially like: "Before you condemn a man you must walk a mile in his moccasins." Think about what that means. If we could actually put on his moccasins, we could walk where he walks, see what he sees, hear what he hears, think his thoughts, and know his problems. This would make a big difference in our attitude toward him.

The Bible tells us we are to love our neighbor. To do this we must understand him. But this takes a lot of effort. It is not easy to understand people who are different from us. We need to take time to study and think about their problems. We need to think what we would do if we lived in the same place and the same circumstances. When we make this extra effort to understand our neighbor, we find that we can, with God's help, love him more easily.

Our neighbors are not just the people who live next to us on our street. In the largest sense our neighbors are the people with whom we share our city, our country, and our world. That makes the Indian our neighbor even if we don't live next door to one. That means that God wants you to love all of the people he has created.

38.

IN GOD WE TRUST

OBJECT: Silver dollar or a large drawing of a coin.

LESSON: What "In God We Trust" means for us and our country.

TEXT: "It is better to trust in the Lord than to depend on man" (Ps. 118:8).

OUTLINE

Introduce object: I have in my hand something all of you are interested in—money.
1. "In" means not on or by but trusting totally in God for all things.
2. "God" means in him alone and not in money or what it can buy.
3. "We" means everybody.
4. "Trust" means complete faith in our creator.
Conclusion: How can you help our country live by this motto?

I have in my hand something all of you are interested in—money. Do you know what people used for money before they had a way of making money like we use today? If you look back far enough in history you can find hundreds of different things that people used to pay for what they wanted: salt, stones, feathers, skulls of animals, jewels, gold, silver, and so on. A man that made shoes could trade them for food or other clothes. A farmer could trade eggs or corn for cooking utensils. The closest thing we have today to that kind of trading is the garage sale or a swap meet.

Every country has its own kind of money. Some countries have very colorful bills. Many coins are slightly different sizes than ours. If you look closely you will be able to tell what country the money comes from. Our money says "The United States of America." This silver dollar also says "In God We Trust." These words were not on our early money but they are on all of our coins and bills now. What do we mean by "In God We Trust"? Let's take a look at the words one at a time.

"In" means that we trust in God completely. It does not say *on* or *by* or *under,* but "In." Our trust should be in God totally—for all things.

"God" means that we trust not in money or what it can buy but in God who loves us and will take care of us.

"We" means everybody—all of us as a nation. Unfortunately, not everybody in our country knows about or trusts in God. If they did, think of how much better everything would be. We could do away with jails—perhaps even poverty. It is important for all of us to pray for our country and its leaders, that they learn to rely on God.

"Trust" means to have complete faith in our Creator. It means we will look to him in every decision that will affect our country.

This is what the people who began our country wanted. Check *your* money. Does it say "In God We Trust"? How can you help our country to live by this motto?

39.

WHAT IN THE WORLD IS THIS!

OBJECT: A carpet beater, or any gadget which is useful but whose purpose is not apparent and one your group has most likely not seen before. Cards with the words "Faith" and "Prayer" printed on them.

LESSON: You can't say whether or not faith and prayer work until you try them.

TEXT: "Find out for yourself how good the Lord is. Happy are those who find safety with him" (Ps. 34:8).

OUTLINE

Introduce object: What do you think this is?

1. You cannot always tell what something is by just looking at it. The words "Faith" and "Prayer" do not tell you what faith and prayer are.
2. You need to be told what it is and how it works. You need to be told about faith and prayer and see it in the lives of others.
3. The real test is to try it for yourself. You'll never know for sure if faith and prayer work until you try them in your own life.

Conclusion: Try it—you'll like it!

What do you think this is? It looks like a funny tennis racquet but it isn't. It looks like a big fly swatter, but it isn't. You hit something with it, but not tennis balls or bugs. Do you give up? You really can't tell from looking at this what it is. I'll have to tell you. It is a carpet beater. It is something people used to keep their rugs cleaned. They put their carpet on a clothesline or a tree and then smacked it with this beater. Dust would fly into the air, and out of the rugs. Does it really work? I can tell you what it is and how it works but you would have to try it for yourself to know for sure.

Do you know what the words on these cards are? If you can't read them, I can tell you what they say. This one says "Faith" and this one says "Prayer." Does that tell you what faith and prayer really are? You can't tell much from just looking at these cards.

I will tell you what faith and prayer are. Faith is believing in God and knowing that he loves you and trusting that he will take care of you. Prayer is communicating with God. You talk to him and know that he hears you and will help you. You can learn about faith and prayer by seeing how they work in the lives of other Christians. They will be happy to tell you about it.

You can learn a lot about faith and prayer this way, but you will never really know if they work until you try them for yourself. Try it—you'll like it!

40.

A FATHER'S LOVE
(FATHER'S DAY)

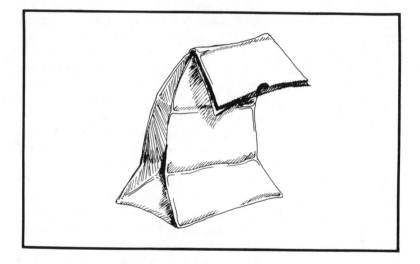

OBJECT: A large, empty bag.

LESSON: Your father is unique. He loves you. Thank him and thank God for him.

TEXT: "Sons, listen to what your father teaches you. Pay attention, and you will have understanding" (Prov. 4:1).

OUTLINE

Introduce object: Would you like to see what is in this bag?
1. Each father is different.
2. The greatest things your father gives you cannot be handled or measured or put into a bag.

Conclusion: Fathers are all different, special, unique. Your father is special to you because he loves you. Thank him for being who he is and for caring for you. Thank God for him!

Would you like to see what is in this bag? It is empty. If you don't believe me I will turn it upside down and shake it. Why would I bring an empty bag? Not to trick you but to help me make my point.

Today I want to talk about fathers. Each father is different. Each father has his own interests and personality. If we were all to fill a bag with things that remind us of our fathers, each bag would be different. I have one empty bag but I want each of you to imagine what you would put in it if this were your bag for your father. Think of all of the different things your father does with and for you. Don't forget the things he teaches you.

Another reason the bag is empty is because the greatest things your father has for you cannot be put into a bag. Your father loves you; he is concerned about you; he prays for you. This love and concern cannot be touched or held up to view. I could not possibly put it into a bag. Even if it cannot be measured, your father shows you this love and concern in many ways.

Your father loves you when he plays with you and takes you places. Your father loves you when he smiles at you because you have made him happy. Your father loves you when he scolds you and punishes you because it is his responsibility to teach you what is right and keep you safe. Your father loves you when he prays with you, tells you about Jesus, and takes you to church.

Fathers are all different, special, unique. Your father is special to you because he loves you. Thank him for being who he is and for caring for you. Thank God for him!

41.

YOU JUST CAN'T GET AWAY

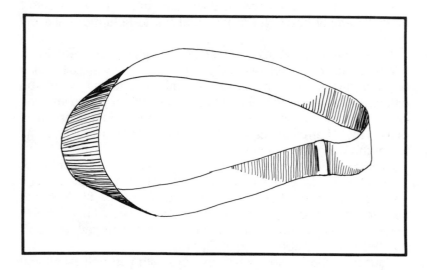

OBJECT: A strip of paper about three inches wide and a yard long. Make a "one-sided" loop by turning one end of the strip around and pasting the two ends together. To cut loop, push scissors into the center of the strip and cut the long way.

LESSON: We are dependent upon, and yet responsible for, each other.

TEXT: "Love one another warmly as Christian brothers, and be eager to show respect for one another" (Rom. 12:10).

OUTLINE

Introduce object: Imagine with me that this strip is two Christians.

1. Cut through strip lengthwise. We cannot separate ourselves from those around us.
2. Cut through the double-length strip you have just made in the same way. You are intertwined, dependent upon, others as well.

Conclusion: God loves us, we love him, and we love each other.

Imagine with me that this strip is two Christians. They sit together in class or church. They share the same goals. They love the same Jesus. The one on this side, however, thinks he wants to be left alone. He wants to be cut off from the others. (Cut lengthwise around the strip, talking as you cut, until you have a double-sized loop.) I'll try to cut this one off. He thinks he doesn't have any responsibility to those around him. He wants to be left alone and not to have to bother with helping others. He's almost cut off. There! Wait a minute—it's still one loop. I tried to cut him off but I couldn't. God has made us responsible for each other. We cannot be separated from those around us.

Let me try cutting the loop again. This time I have a person who thinks he can take care of himself. He says he doesn't need any help from anybody. (Cut the double loop lengthwise in the same way again, talking as you cut.) I wonder what will happen when we get him cut off. There! Hm, now I have two loops that are hooked together. God has made us dependent on each other for love, encouragement, and fellowship. Christians have a strong bond. God loves us, we love him, and we love each other.

42.

WHEN IS A BEAR NOT A BEAR?

OBJECT: A stuffed animal shaped like a koala, or a large picture of a koala.

LESSON: We need spiritual nourishment.

TEXT: "All ate the same spiritual bread and drank the same spiritual drink. They drank from the spiritual rock that went with them; and that was Christ himself" (I Cor. 10:3, 4).

OUTLINE

Introduce object: When is a bear not a bear? When it is a koala.
1. Its pouch makes the koala different. Our desire to follow Jesus makes us different.
2. The koala needs a special diet. We need food for our spiritual nature.
3. The koala is a protected species. We are protected by God.
Conclusion: Our wise God knows our needs.

When is a bear not a bear? When it is a koala. A koala looks like a bear, but it is really a kind of animal called a *marsupial,* which means an animal that carries its young in its pouch. Can you think of another animal that carries its young in its pouch? The kangaroo does. There is something that makes Christians different, also. They all desire to follow Jesus.

The koala has a large, flat, black nose. It also has sharp claws to help it climb the eucalyptus trees in Australia. The Koala spends much time in the eucalyptus tree because the leaves and shoots of this tree are its only food. It doesn't even drink water. It gets its moisture from the leaves.

The part of us that thinks and feels and wants to follow Jesus needs special food also. It needs to study God's word, to pray, and to think about the Christian life. It needs to think about things that are pure and good. Just as the koala will die if it is taken away from the eucalyptus tree, so too will our Christian love and joy slowly die if it is not fed spiritual food.

For a long time people in Australia hunted the koala for its soft fur. But the Australian government didn't want all of the koalas to be caught, so it passed laws saying that people may not hunt the koala. Since the koala is protected by the government, it is called a protected species. We are also a protected species. God cares for us. He keeps us from harm. Our wise God knows our needs.